Learning SQL
in SQLite for Beginners

Djoni Darmawikarta

Table of Contents

Introduction...6
   Software Requirements 6
Chapter 1 Storing and Maintaining Data........................8
   Creating Database and Preparing SQL Editor 8
   Creating Tables 15
   Adding Data 18
      NULL 21
   Updating Data 22
   Deleting Data 24
   Summary 27
Chapter 2: Queries...28
   The SELECT statement...28
   Querying All Data..28
   Selecting Specific Columns 29
   Selecting Rows with WHERE 30
   Compound Conditions 32
   Evaluation Precedence and Parentheses............................34
   The NOT logical operator 35
   The BETWEEN Operator 37
   The IN Operator 37
   The LIKE Operator 38
   Escape 39
   Combining the NOT operator 41
   Handling NULL 41
   Summary 42
Chapter 3: Query Output..43
   Column Aliases 43
   Expressions 44
   Ordering Output Rows 46
      Ordering by One Column...47
      Direction of Order...47
      Multiple Columns..49

Different Directions on Different Columns 50
Ordering with a WHERE clause 50
Limit without offset..52
Limit with Where 53
LIMIT with ORDER BY 54
The DISTINCT Keyword 56
Aggregate Functions 57
The CASE expression 59
Simple CASE 59
Searched CASE 60
Storing Query Output 62
Summary 64
Chapter 4 Grouping..**65**
The GROUP BY Clause..65
Grouping on more than one column..66
HAVING Keyword 69
Summary 71
Chapter 5 Joins **72**
Additional tables required for the examples 72
Using Table Aliases 74
Joining More than Two Tables 75
Joining on More than One Column..77
Left Outer Join..**79**
Rows with NULL only..80
Self-Joins **81**
The USING Keyword 83
Summary..**84**
Chapter 6 Compound Queries..**85**
UNION ALL 85
UNION..87
INTERSECT..88
EXCEPT..89
Summary 91
Chapter 7 Subqueries..**92**
Single-Row Subquery 92
Multiple-row subquery..93

First Row..95
IN and NOT IN 95
Nested Subqueries..97
Correlated Subqueries 98
Summary 100
Appendix A: Command-line Shell..101

Introduction

Most applications store their data in databases. Most of their databases are relational. SQLite is one of the most-used relational databases. It is an open source database that you can download from https://www.sqlite.org/index.html

To access data in a relational database we use SQL (Structured Query Language).

If you are new to SQL and/or SQLite database, this is the book of choice.

It is a practical book, teaching you SQL step-by-step using examples. If you take a glance at the table of contents, you will appreciate the comprehensive coverage of the book.

When you finish the book, you'd be ready to apply your SQL skill in real-world projects.

Software Requirements

I wrote and tested the book examples in **SQLiteStudio**. SQLiteStudio is an open source GUI for specifically working with SQLite database. The SQL statement and its result are shown in this book as SQLiteStudio screenshots. So, in addition to SQLite, you will want to have an installation of SQLiteStudio. You can download SQLiteStudio from https://sqlitestudio.pl/

If you want to you can type and execute the SQL statements of the book examples in the **SQLite command-line shell** window. SQLite command-line shell is an SQLite tool that you can also download from the SQLite web site. If you are curious about it, consult Appendix A: Command-line shell.

Here's a screenshot of a part of the SQLite download page. I downloaded the last two items highlighted in red for my writing this book. The first item is SQLite database and the second item has the command-line tools, which includes the Command-line shell.

SQLite Download Page

Source Code

sqlite-amalgamation-3390200.zip (2.44 MiB)   C source code as an amalgamation, version 3.39.2.
(sha1: deb2abefa17b4505525e381a2b09a5dc069fb62f2f02e4d1b408ba5f41990ca7)

sqlite-autoconf-3390200.tar.gz (2.92 MiB)   C source code as an amalgamation. Also includes a "configure" script and TEA makefiles for the TCL Interface.
(sha3: b095801eb33705451eb1c6718b8ec3103e085a613c4824a076ca31c6a4bc5bee)

Documentation

sqlite-doc-3390200.zip (10.19 MiB)   Documentation as a bundle of static HTML files.
(sha3: 22035ebc460399356663bc38310c791aa7a64fbae23f94c9aedf96d45461bdb14)

Precompiled Binaries for Android

sqlite-android-3390200.aar (3.22 MiB)   A precompiled Android library containing the core SQLite together with appropriate Java bindings, ready to drop into any Android Studio project.
(sha1: c7f6275a628ae948a412ed27c35057fb67a87e418a536ac84cc1a7e1849ec52)

Precompiled Binaries for Linux

sqlite-tools-linux-x86-3390200.zip (2.14 MiB)   A bundle of command-line tools for managing SQLite database files, including the command-line shell program, the sqldiff program, and the sqlite3_analyzer program.
(sha1: db5772065ec251c8c273e6a831f15e28cebb31ca91032f5135a0998f1659b3a11)

Precompiled Binaries for Mac OS X (x86)

sqlite-tools-osx-x86-3390200.zip (1.52 MiB)   A bundle of command-line tools for managing SQLite database files, including the command-line shell program, the sqldiff program, and the sqlite3_analyzer program.
(sha3: 29f7c487ef047dda1310c4e5e03fbdce02525ab4421d8852b431e0310eae455ac)

Precompiled Binaries for Windows

sqlite-dll-win32-x86-3390200.zip (557.47 KiB)   32-bit DLL (x86) for SQLite version 3.39.2.
(sha3: d8f04a09a1c92360b4ae1717a24e45331a102a903dd6578f6b941421dcd3e441)

sqlite-dll-win64-x64-3390200.zip (893.05 KiB)   64-bit DLL (x64) for SQLite version 3.39.2.
(sha3: 1ea0b30ec3a75d4f99f75420bdbacbf19c76099a68d16c2dbcb4a09629cafdeb0)

sqlite-tools-win32-x86-3390200.zip (1.88 MiB)   A bundle of command-line tools for managing SQLite database files, including the command-line shell program, the sqldiff.exe program, and the sqlite3_analyzer.exe program.
(sha3: 4b1f487cb1bf8bcdf0a1e42c9ec50773ede13433b05cdb0a082a640519196c34)

Precompiled Binaries for .NET

Chapter 1 Storing and Maintaining Data

Data in SQLite is stored in tables. A sales database, for example, might have four tables for storing product, customer, suppliers, and customer order data.

When you add a record of data into a table, the record is stored as a row of the table. A record has fields. A product record, for example, might have four fields: product code, name, price, and launch date. All records you store in the product table must have the same fields. Each of the fields is a column of the table.

You will, in this chapter, learn the SQL statements to create a database and tables in the database, then store and maintain data.

To learn the most, please try the examples.

Creating Database and Preparing SQL Editor

You will create a new sales database and get your SQLiteStudio ready for your SQL practice.

Follow the steps below:

1. Start SQLiteStudio.
2. To create a new database, click the Add a Database icon shown highlighted in red in the screenshot below.

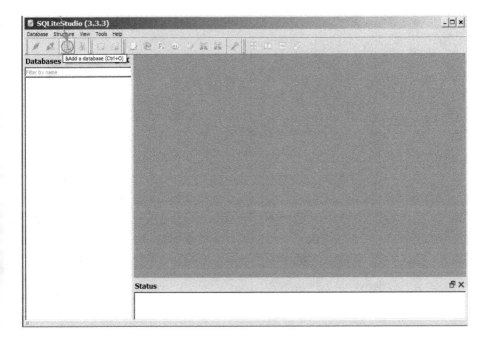

3. On the pop-up Database window, click the Create new database file.

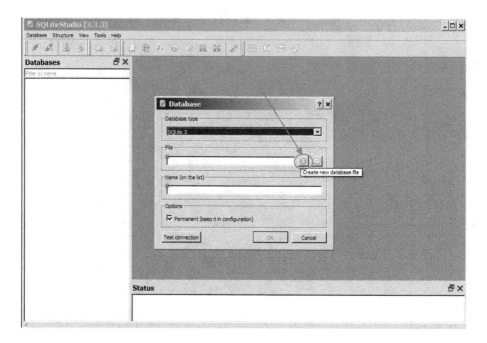

4. Go to the folder where you want to store the database file, type sales.db as the file name, and click the Save button.

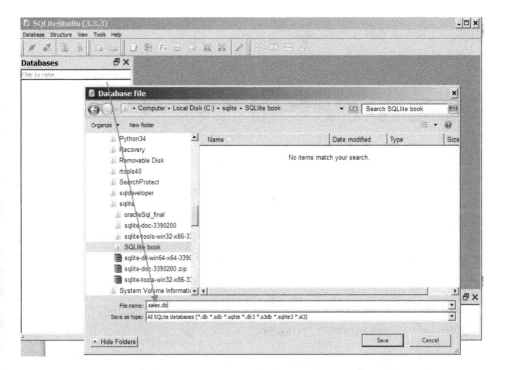

5. Back on the Database window, click the Test connection button and if connection is good you will see a green check. Click the OK button, the Database window will get closed.

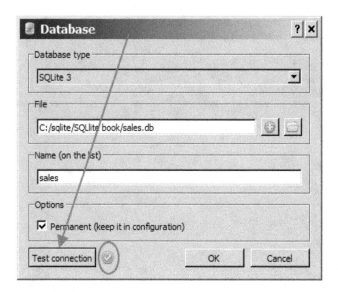

6. You will now see the sales database listed on the Databases panel of your SQLiteStudio main window.

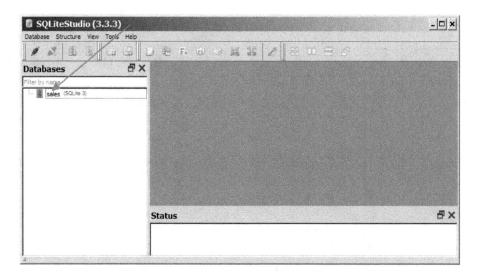

7. Right click the sales database, and select Connect to the database.

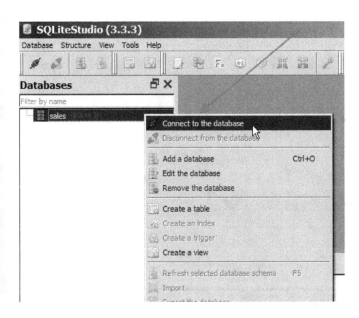

8. Click Open SQL Editor.

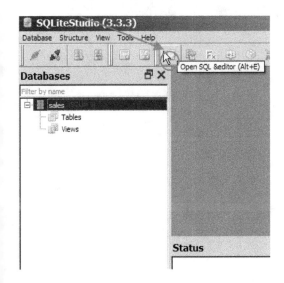

Your SQLiteStudio is now ready for entering and executing SQL
statements, which you will do to try following the book examples.

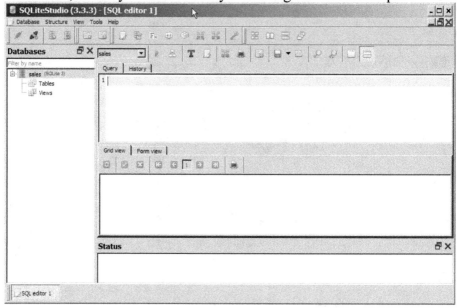

Creating Tables

We use the SQL statement CREATE TABLE to create tables.

The syntax of the CREATE TABLE statement is as follows.

```
CREATE TABLE tablename
    (column_1 data_type_1,
     column_2 data_type_2,
     ...
     PRIMARY KEY (columns)
);
```

Example 1.1 shows a CREATE TABLE statement for creating a product table with four columns. We designate the p_code column as the primary key of the product table, as we want product data (rows of the table) to be unique on their p_code, i.e. no two product (rows) can have the same p_code. Also, as a primary key p_code must have a value, cannot be null.

Example 1.1: Creating product table

```
CREATE TABLE product
   ( p_code    INT,
     p_name    TEXT,
     price     REAL,
     launch_dt TEXT,
     PRIMARY KEY (p_code)
   );
```

The four columns have three different data types:

INT is for storing signed integer
TEXT for characters
REAL for floating point number

An SQL statement must be terminated with a semicolon (;)

Please type in the SQL statement. You can press the Format button to tidy up your SQL statement; your lines of code will get aligned and SQL keywords capitalized.

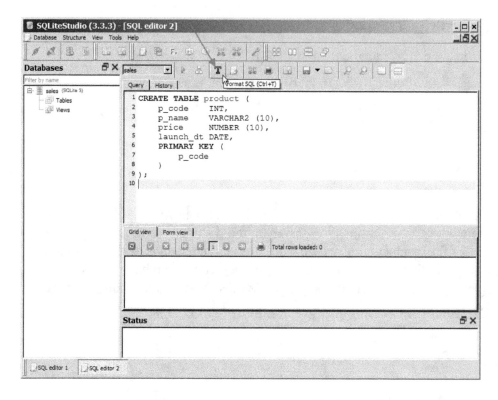

When you run the SQL statement by pressing F9, the product table is created. To see the product table, click the expand +

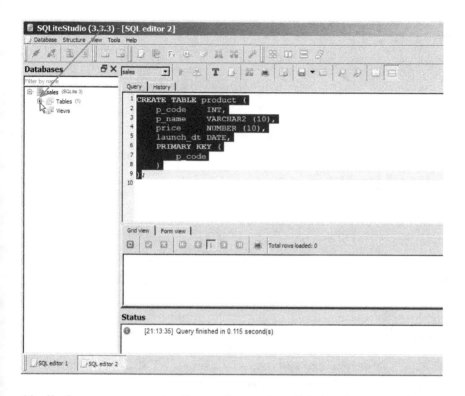

Similarly you can see the four columns by clicking the expand +

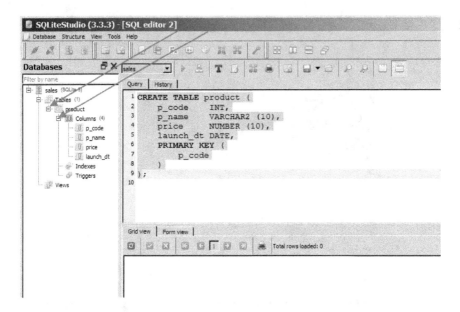

Adding Data

Once you have a table, you can add data to it using the INSERT statement. The syntax for the INSERT statement is as follows.

```
INSERT INTO table
    (column_1,
     column_2,
     ... )
VALUES (value_1,
        value_2,
     ... )
);
```

The SQL statement in Example 1.2 inserts a row into the product table. Make sure your cursor is on the insert statement and press F9 to execute the statement.

Example 1.2: Adding a row into the product table

```
INSERT INTO product VALUES (1, 'Nail', 10.0, '2013-03-31');
```

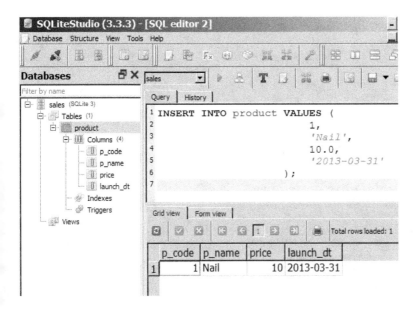

After executing the statement, the product table will have one row. You can check the row using this statement.

```
SELECT * FROM product;
```

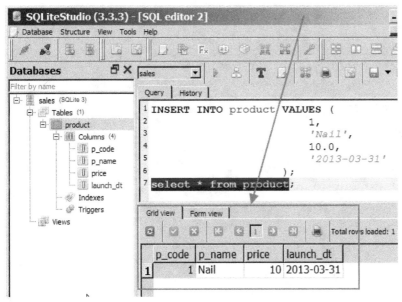

To insert more than one row, use the following syntax.

```
INSERT INTO table1 (column1, column2, ...)
VALUES
    (value1, value2, ...),
    (value1, value2, ...),
    ...
    (value1, value2, ...);
```

Example 1.3 adds five more rows to the product table.

Example 1.3: Adding five more rows

```
INSERT INTO product (p_code, p_name, price, launch_dt)
  VALUES (2, 'Washer', 15.00, '2013-03-29'),
  (3, 'Nut', 15.00, '2013-03-29'),
  (4, 'Screw', 25.00, '2013-03-30'),
  (5, 'Super_Nut', 30.00, '2013-03-30'),
  (6, 'New Nut', NULL, NULL);
```

After executing the statement in Example 1.3, your product table will contain a total of six rows as shown below.

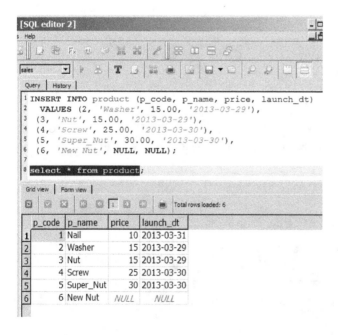

NULL

NULL indicates an absence of a data; it is neither 0 (zero) or empty. Chapter 2, "Basic Queries" has a section ("Handling NULL") that explains NULL in detail.

Updating Data

You use the UPDATE statement to update one or more columns of existing data. You can update all rows in a table or certain rows in the table.

The syntax for the UPDATE statement is as follows

```
UPDATE table_name
SET column_1 = new_value_1 [,
    column_2 = new_value_2,
    ... ]
[WHERE condition];
```

You specify which rows to update in the WHERE clause. Without a WHERE clause, all rows will be updated. With a WHERE clause, only rows that meet the condition will be updated. If no row meets the condition in the WHERE clause, nothing will be updated.

As an example, the SQL statement in Example 1.4 will reduce the price by 5%. As the UPDATE statement does not have a WHERE clause, the prices of all the products will be updated.

Example 1.4: Updating the price column

```
UPDATE product SET price = price - (price * 0.05);
```

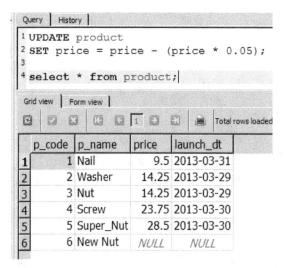

22

Example 1.5 will update the price of only the product with p_code = 9, its price is reduced by 0.5. But, as there's no row with p_code = 9, no row gets updated.

Example 1.5: Updating the price column with a WHERE clause

```
UPDATE product SET price = price - 0.5
WHERE p_code = 9;
```

Query | History |

```
1 UPDATE product SET price = price * 0.5
2 WHERE p_code = 9;
3
4 select * from product;|        I
```

Grid view | Form view |

Total rows loaded: 6

	p_code	p_name	price	launch_dt
1	1	Nail	9.5	2013-03-31
2	2	Washer	14.25	2013-03-29
3	3	Nut	14.25	2013-03-29
4	4	Screw	23.75	2013-03-30
5	5	Super_Nut	28.5	2013-03-30
6	6	New Nut	NULL	NULL

Deleting Data

To delete a row or multiple rows in a table, use the DELETE statement. You can specify which rows to be deleted by using the WHERE clause.

The syntax for the DELETE statement is as follows

```
DELETE FROM table
[WHERE condition];
```

You specify which rows to delete in the WHERE clause.

For example, the statement in Example 1.6 deletes from the product table all rows whose p_name field value is 'Nut'.

Example 1.6: Deleting rows

```
DELETE FROM product
WHERE p_name = 'Nut';
```

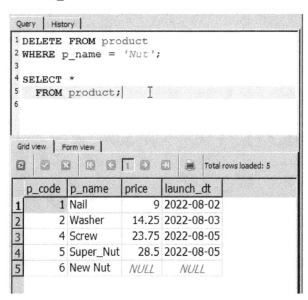

If none of the rows meets the condition, nothing will be deleted. See Example 1.7.

Example 1.7: No product got deleted

```
DELETE FROM product WHERE price = 10;
```

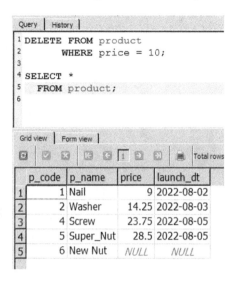

Without the WHERE condition, all rows will be deleted and the product table will be empty. When run the SQL statement in Example 1.8 all rows will be deleted.

Example 1.8: Deleting all rows

```
DELETE FROM product;
```

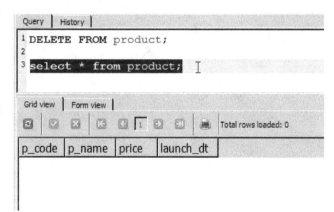

Let's add back the original six rows. Execute the INSERT statement in Example 1.9.

Example 1.9: (Re)inserting all six rows

```
INSERT INTO product (p_code, p_name, price, launch_dt)
  VALUES (1, 'Nail', 10.0, '2013-03-31'),
  (2, 'Washer', 15.00, '2013-03-29'),
  (3, 'Nut', 15.00, '2013-03-29'),
  (4, 'Screw', 25.00, '2013-03-30'),
  (5, 'Super_Nut', 30.00, '2013-03-30'),
  (6, 'New Nut', NULL, NULL);
```

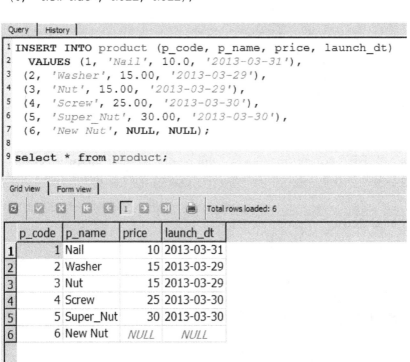

Summary

In this chapter you got the first taste of working with SQL. You learned how to create a table, store and maintain data. In Chapter 2, "Basic Queries" you will learn to use the SELECT statement to query data.

Chapter 2: Queries

A query is a request for data from one or more tables. When you execute a query, rows satisfying the condition of the query will be returned as a table. Similarly, when a query embedded in another query or a program gets executed, the data returned to the other query or the program is a table.

In this chapter you learn how to write basic queries using the SELECT statement.

The SELECT statement

All queries regardless of their complexity use the SELECT statement. The SELECT statement has the following general syntax.

```
SELECT column_names FROM table_name [WHERE condition];
```

Only the SELECT and FROM clauses are mandatory. If your query does not have a WHERE clause, the result will include all rows in the table. If your query has a WHERE clause then only the rows satisfying the WHERE condition will be returned.

Querying All Data

The simplest query, which reads all data (all rows and all columns) from a table, has the following syntax.

```
SELECT * FROM table;
```

The asterisk (*) means all columns in the table. For instance, Example 2.1 shows an SQL statement that queries all data from the product table.

Example 2.1: Querying all product data

```
SELECT * FROM product;
```

Executing the query will give you the following result.

Selecting Specific Columns

To query specific columns, list the columns in the SELECT clause. You write the columns in the order you want to see them in the output table. For example, the SELECT statement in Example 2.2 queries the p_name and the price columns from the product table.

Example 2.2: Querying specific columns

```
SELECT p_name, price FROM product;
```

All rows containing p_name and price columns will be returned by the query.

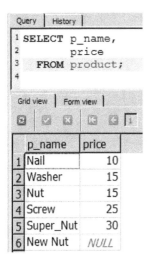

Selecting Rows with WHERE

To query specific rows, use the WHERE clause. Recall that the SQL SELECT statement has the following syntax.

```
SELECT column_names FROM table_name [WHERE condition];
```

For example, the SQL statement in Example 2.3 queries the p_name and price data from the product table with price = 15.

Example 2.3: Querying specific rows

```
SELECT p_name, price FROM product WHERE price = 15;
```

Only rows with price = 15 will be returned by the query, in this case the Washer and Nut.

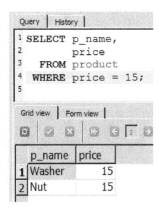

The equal sign (=) in the WHERE condition in Example 2.3 is one of the comparison operators. Table 2.1 shows all comparison operators.

Operator	Description
=	Equal to
<	Less than
>	Greater than
<=	Less than or equal to
>=	Greater than or equal to
!=	Not equal to

Table 2.1: Comparison operators

Example 2.4 shows a WHERE clause that uses the not equal to (!=) operator.

Example 2.4: Using the != comparison operator

```
SELECT p_name, price FROM product WHERE p_name != 'Nail';
```

Only rows whose p_name is not Nail will be returned by the query.

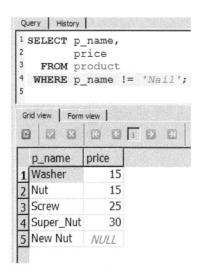

Compound Conditions

The condition p_name != 'Nail' in Example 2.4 is called a predicate. Using the AND and OR logical operator you can combine predicates to form a compound condition. Only rows that satisfy the compound condition will be returned by the query.

The rules for the OR logical operator are given in Table 2.2.

Left condition	Logical operator	Right condition	Compound condition
True	OR	True	True
True	OR	False	True
False	OR	True	True
False	OR	False	False

Table 2.2: The OR rules

In principle, the result of the OR compound condition is true (satisfying the condition) if any one of the two conditions being OR-ed is true; otherwise, if none of the conditions is true, the compound condition is false (not satisfying the condition).

The rules for the AND logical operator are presented in Table 2.3.

Left	Logical	Right	Compound

condition	operator	condition	condition
True	AND	True	True
True	AND	False	FALSE
False	AND	True	FALSE
False	AND	False	FALSE

Table 2.3: The AND rules

Basically, the result of the AND compound condition is true only if the two conditions being AND-ed are true; otherwise, the result is false.

For example, the statement in Example 2.5 contains three predicates in its WHERE clause.

Example 2.5: A query with three predicates

```
SELECT *
FROM product
WHERE (launch_dt >= '2013-03-30'
OR price        > 15)
AND (p_name     != 'Nail');
```

The result of the first compound condition (launch_dt >= '2013-03-31' OR price > 15) is true for Nail, Screw and Super_Nut rows in the product table; AND-ing this result with the (p_name != 'Nail') predicate results in two products, the Screw and Super_Nut.

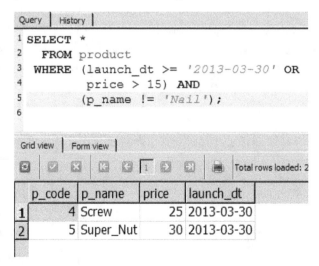

Note that New Nut does not satisfy the condition because applying any of the comparison operators to NULL results in false (the price and launch_dt of the New Nut are NULL). The section "Handling NULL" later in this chapter explains more about NULL.

Evaluation Precedence and Parentheses

If a compound condition contains both the OR condition and the AND condition, the AND condition will be evaluated first because AND has a higher precedence than OR. However, anything in parentheses will have an even higher precedence than AND. For example, the SELECT statement in Example 2.5 has an OR and an AND, but the OR condition is in parentheses so the OR condition is evaluated first. If you remove the parentheses in the SELECT statement in Example 2.5, the query will return a different result.

Consider the statement in Example 2.6, which is similar to that in Example 2.5 except that the parentheses have been removed.

Example 2.6: Evaluation precedence

```
SELECT *
FROM product
WHERE launch_dt >= '2013-03-30'
OR price        > 15
AND p_name      != 'Nail';
```

Without the parentheses, the compound condition price > 15 AND p_name != 'Nail' will be evaluated first, resulting in the Screw and Super_Nut. The result is then OR-ed with the launch_dt >= 2022-08-01' condition, resulting in an additional row, the Nail, hence the query output is three rows.

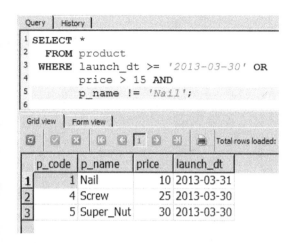

The NOT logical operator

You can use NOT to negate a condition and return rows that do not satisfy the condition. Consider the query in Example 2.7.

Example 2.7: Using the NOT operator

```
SELECT *
FROM product
WHERE NOT (launch_dt >= '30-MAR-13'
OR price          > 15
AND p_name        != 'Nail');
```

Thanks to the NOT operator in the query in Example 2.7, the two rows not satisfying the condition in Example 2.6 will now be returned.

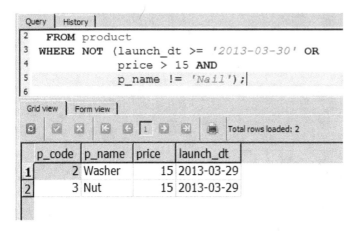

As another example, the query in Example 2.8 negates the last predicate only (as opposed to the previous query that negated the overall WHERE condition).

Example 2.8: Using NOT on one predicate

```
SELECT *
FROM product
WHERE (launch_dt >= '2013-03-30'
OR price          > 15)
AND NOT (p_name != 'Nail');
```

The output of the query in Example 2.8 is as follows.

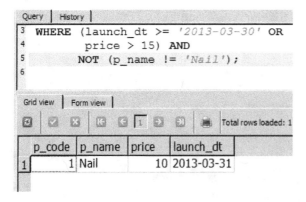

The BETWEEN Operator

The BETWEEN operator evaluates equality to any value within a range. The range is specified by a boundary, which specifies the lowest and the highest values.

Here is the syntax for BETWEEN.

```
SELECT columns FROM table
WHERE column BETWEEN(lowest_value, highest_value);
```

The boundary values are inclusive, meaning *lowest_value* and *highest_value* will be included in the equality evaluation.

For example, the query in Example 2.9 uses the BETWEEN operator to specify the lowest and highest prices that need to be returned from the product table.

Example 2.9: Using the BETWEEN operator

```
SELECT * FROM product WHERE price BETWEEN 15 AND 25;
```

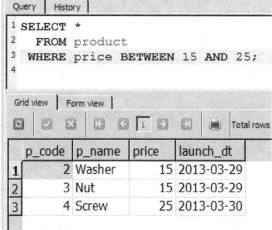

The IN Operator

The IN operator compares a column with a list of values. The syntax for a query that uses IN is as follows.

```
SELECT columns FROM table
```

```
WHERE column IN(value1, value2, ...);
```

For example, the query in Example 2.10 uses the IN operator to select all columns whose price is in the list (10, 25, 50).

Example 2.10: Using the IN operator

```
SELECT * FROM product WHERE price IN (10, 25, 50);
```

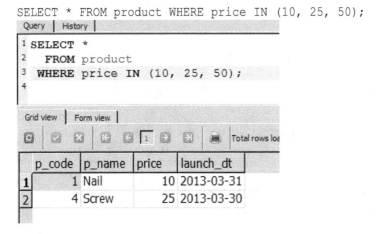

The LIKE Operator

The LIKE operator allows you to specify an imprecise equality condition. The syntax is as follows.

```
SELECT columns FROM table
WHERE column LIKE ' ... wildcard_character ... ';
```

The wildcard character can be a percentage sign (%) to represent any number of characters or an underscore (_) to represent a single occurrence of any character.

As an example, the query in Example 2.11 uses the LIKE operator to find products whose name starts with N and is followed by two other characters plus products whose name starts with Sc and can be of any length.

Example 2.11: Using the LIKE operator

```
SELECT * FROM product WHERE p_name LIKE 'N__' OR p_name LIKE 'Sc%';
```

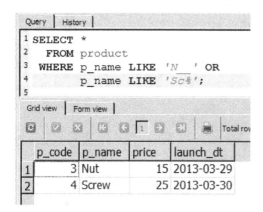

Even though you can use LIKE for numeric columns, it is primarily used with columns of type string.

Escape

If the string you specify in the LIKE operator contains an underscore or a percentage sign, SQL will regard it as a wild character. For example, if you want to query products that have an underscore in their names, your SQL statement would look like that in Example 2.12.

Example 2.12: A wildcard character _ in the LIKE string

```
SELECT * FROM product WHERE p_name LIKE '%_%';
```

Executing the query in Example 2.12 will return all rows instead of just the Super_Nut, because the underscore in the LIKE operator is regarded as a wild card character, i.e. any one character.

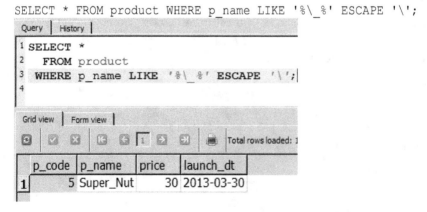

```
Query  History
1 SELECT *
2   FROM product
3 WHERE p_name LIKE '%_%';
4
```

Grid view | Form view

Total rows l

p_code	p_name	price	launch_dt
1	Nail	10	2013-03-31
2	Washer	15	2013-03-29
3	Nut	15	2013-03-29
4	Screw	25	2013-03-30
5	Super_Nut	30	2013-03-30
6	New Nut	NULL	NULL

Example 2.13 resolves this problem by prefixing the wild card character with an ESCAPE character. In the statement the ESCAPE clause defines \ (backslash) as an escape character, meaning any character in the LIKE operator after a backslash will be considered a character, not as a wildcard character. Now only rows whose p_name contains an underscore will be returned.

Example 2.13: Escaping the wildcard character _

```
SELECT * FROM product WHERE p_name LIKE '%\_%' ESCAPE '\';
```

```
Query  History
1 SELECT *
2   FROM product
3 WHERE p_name LIKE '%\_%' ESCAPE '\';
4
```

Grid view | Form view

Total rows loaded: 1

p_code	p_name	price	launch_dt
5	Super_Nut	30	2013-03-30

40

Combining the NOT operator

You can combine NOT with BETWEEN, IN, or LIKE to negate their conditions. For example, the query in Example 2.14 uses NOT with BETWEEN.

Example 2.14: Using **NOT** with **BETWEEN**

```
SELECT * FROM product WHERE price NOT BETWEEN 15 AND 25;
```

	Query	History

```
1 SELECT *
2   FROM product
3 WHERE price NOT BETWEEN 15 AND 25;
4
```

Grid view	Form view

Total rows loaded:

	p_code	p_name	price	launch_dt
1	1	Nail	10	2013-03-31
2	5	Super_Nut	30	2013-03-30

Handling NULL

NULL, an SQL reserved word, represents the absence of data. NULL is applicable to any data type. It is not the same as a numeric zero or an empty string or a 0000/00/00 date. You can specify whether or not a column can be null in the CREATE TABLE statement for creating the table.

The result of applying any of the comparison operators on NULL is always NULL. You can only test whether or not a column is NULL by using the IS NULL or IS NOT NULL operator.

Consider the query in Example 2.15.

Example 2.15: Invalid usage of the equal operator on **NULL**

```
SELECT * FROM product WHERE price = NULL;
```

Executing the query in Example 2.15 produces no output. In fact, you will get the following message.

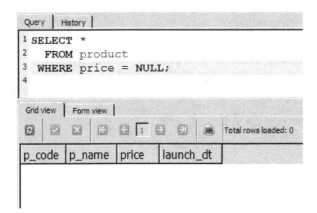

The query in Example 2.16 uses IS NULL, and we get the expected result: the New Nut as its price is NULL.

Example 2.16: Using **IS NULL**

```
SELECT * FROM product WHERE price IS NULL;
```

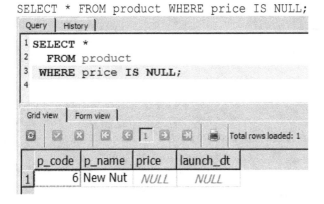

Note

Chapter 6, "Built-in Functions," discusses functions that you can use to test column nullity.

Summary

In this chapter you learned queries using the SELECT statement. In the next chapter you will learn how to format query outputs.

Chapter 3: Query Output

All queries you have learned so far returned rows that contained columns from the source table. However, output rows can also contain string or numeric expressions that include string or numeric literals, operators, and functions.

In this chapter you learn how to manipulate query output using expressions and how to order and store output rows into a table.

Column Aliases

By default the names of the output columns in the query output are the names of the columns of the queried table. However, you don't have to be stuck with the original column names. You can give them different names or aliases if you wish.

The syntax for the SELECT clause that uses aliases is as follows.

```
SELECT column_1 AS alias1, column_2 AS alias2, ...
FROM table;
```

An alias can consist of one or multiple words. You must enclose a multiword alias with square braces, e.g. [PRODUCT NAME]. For example, the query in Example 3.1 uses an alias for the p_name column.

Example 3.1: Using an alias in a query

```
SELECT p_code,
  p_name AS "PRODUCT NAME"
FROM product;
```

```
Query | History |
1 SELECT p_code,
2         p_name AS [PRODUCT NAME]
3   FROM product;
4
```

Grid view | Form view |

	p_code	PRODUCT NAME
1	1	Nail
2	2	Washer
3	3	Nut
4	4	Screw
5	5	Super_Nut
6	6	New Nut

Expressions

An output column can also be an expression. An expression in the SELECT clause can include columns, literal values, arithmetic or string operators, and functions. For instance, the SELECT clause in the query in Example 3.2 employs several expressions.

Example 3.2: Various types of output columns

```
SELECT p_code,
p_name,
'p_name in Uppercase: ' || UPPER(p_name) AS [PRODUCT NAME],--
product name in uppercases
price,
(price * 100) AS NORMALIZED_PRICE,-- price of 100 units
date('now') AS [CURRENT_DATE],-- current date as a string
launch_dt,
strftime('%Y', 'now') - strftime('%Y', launch_dt) AS [YEARS
SINCE LAUNCHED]-- number of years since launch year
FROM product;
```

The output of the query in Example 3.2 will have eight columns. Four of them are columns from table: p_code, p_name, price, and launch_dt. The other four are as follows:

The third column PRODUCT NAME is an expression that contains three parts, a literal 'p_name in Uppercase: ', a concatenation string operator (||), and UPPER(p_name). The latter, UPPER, is a function applied to the p_name column from the product table. The UPPER function changes the case of the product names to uppercase.

NORMALIZED_PRICE column is an arithmetic expression (price*100).

Next column, CURRENT_DATE, is generated by the date function, date('now') generates current date as a string.

The last column, YEARS SINCE LAUNCHED is a calculation, subtraction of current year from launch year. strftime('Y%', 'now') produces the current year and similarly strftime('Y%', launch_dt) produces the year of the launch_dt column.

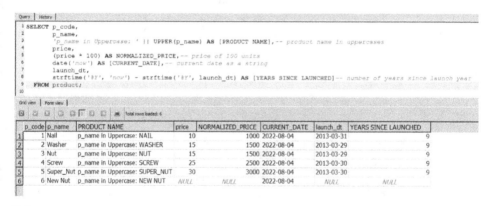

Note

The functions we used in this example are all built-in functions. Chapter 9, "Built-in Functions" explains functions in more detail.

Ordering Output Rows

To provide better visualization of the output, you can order output rows based on certain criteria. To order the output, use the ORDER BY clause. The ORDER BY clause must appear last in a SELECT statement.

Here is the syntax for a query having the ORDER BY clause.

```
SELECT columns
FROM table
WHERE condition
ORDER BY column(s)
```

You can order output rows in one of the following methods.

- by one or more columns
- in ascending or descending direction
- by using the GROUP BY clause
- by using UNION and other set operators

Each of the methods is explained in the subsections below.

Ordering by One Column

To order the output rows, use the ORDER BY clause. The query in Example 3.3 orders the output rows by the product name alphabetically. Note that without the order clause the rows will be in the order they were entered into the table, as shown on the SQL editor 2 panel (the right panel)

Example 3.3: Ordering by one column

```
SELECT * FROM product ORDER BY p_name;
```

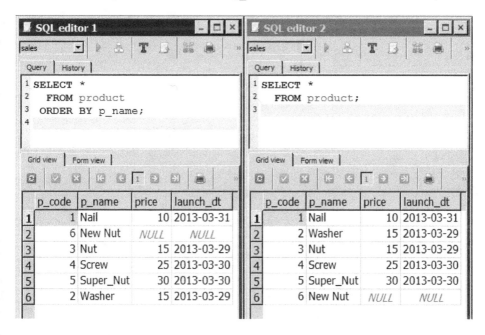

Direction of Order

The default direction is ascending. To order a column in descending direction, use the DESC reserved word. For example, the query in Example 3.4 is similar to that in Example 3.4 except that the output is presented in descending order.

Example 3.4: Changing the order direction

```
SELECT * FROM product ORDER BY p_name DESC;
```

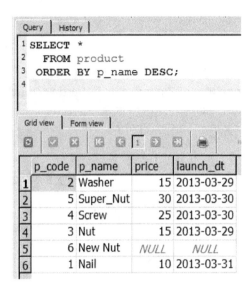

Multiple Columns

To order by more than one column, list the columns in the ORDER BY clause. The sequence of columns listed is significant. The order will be conducted by the first column in the list, followed by the second column, and so on. For example, if the ORDER BY clause has two columns, the query output will first be ordered by the first column. Any rows with identical values in the first column will be further ordered by the second column.

For example, the query in Example 3.5 uses an ORDER BY clause with two columns.

Example 3.5: Multiple column ordering

```
SELECT * FROM product ORDER BY launch_dt, price;
```

The output rows will first be ordered by launch_dt and then by price, both in ascending order. The secondary ordering by price is seen on the Screw and Super_Nut rows. Their launch_dt's are the same, 30-MAR-13. Their prices are different, Screw's lower than Super_Nut's, hence Screw row comes before the Super_Nut.

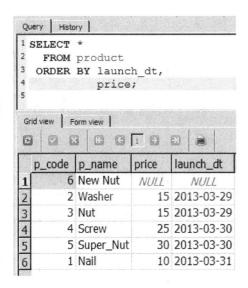

Different Directions on Different Columns

You can apply different order directions on ordered columns too. For example, the query in Example 3.6 uses different directions on different columns in its ORDER BY clause.

Example 3.6: Using multiple directions of ORDER

```
SELECT * FROM product ORDER BY launch_dt, price DESC;
```

Applying the query against the product table, the output rows will be ordered by launch_dt in ascending order and then by price in descending order. Now, the Super_Nut comes before the Screw.

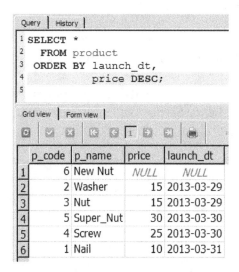

Ordering with a WHERE clause

If your SELECT statement has both the WHERE clause and the ORDER BY clause, ORDER BY must appear after the WHERE clause.

For example, the query in Example 3.7 has both WHERE and ORDER BY. This query will return only Nut products.

Example 3.7: Using both WHERE and ORDER BY

```
SELECT * FROM product WHERE p_name = 'Nut'
ORDER BY p_name, p_code DESC;
```

If you execute the query, you will see one row only, the Nut, in the output window.

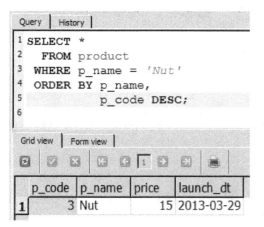

Limiting the Number of Rows

You can limit the number of output row by using the LIMIT clause.

Its syntax is as follows.

```
SELECT column_list
FROM table
LIMIT offset, row_count;
```

Try the query in Example 3.8, which skips the first two rows and gives you the next three rows.

Example 3.8: LIMIT clause

```
SELECT * FROM product LIMIT 2, 3;
```

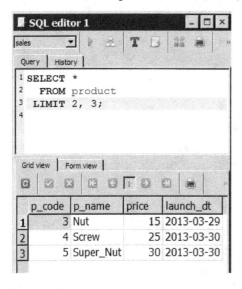

Limit without offset

The offset is optional, without it there'll be no skipping. Please try Example 3.9.

Example 3.9: Limit without offset

```
SELECT * FROM product LIMIT 3;
```

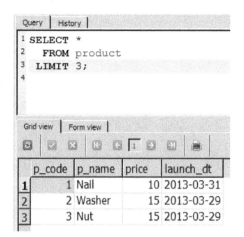

Offset = 0 is similar; no rows will be skipped, as demonstrated in Example 3.5.

Example 3.10: offset = 0

```
SELECT * FROM product LIMIT 0, 3;
```

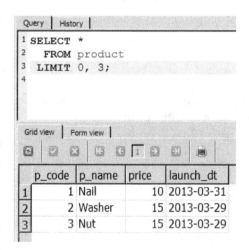

Limit with Where

Your query can have the WHERE condition. It must be before the LIMIT clause. Try Example 3.11.

Example 3.11: with WHERE condition

```
SELECT * FROM product
WHERE price > 15 OR price IS NULL
LIMIT 2;
```

Query	History

```
1 SELECT *
2    FROM product
3  WHERE price > 15 OR
4          price IS NULL
5  LIMIT 2;
6
```

Grid view	Form view

	p_code	p_name	price	launch_dt
1	4	Screw	25	2013-03-30
2	5	Super_Nut	30	2013-03-30

LIMIT with ORDER BY

ORDER BY must be before the LIMIT. The output rows are ordered and only then pick up the rows as specified by the LIMIT, as demonstrated in Example 3.12. The left panel of the screenshot is without the LIMIT producing three rows and then the query with LIMIT, on the right panel, picks up the first two rows.

Example 3.12: Effect of ORDER BY

```
SELECT * FROM product
WHERE price > 15 OR price IS NULL
ORDER BY p_name
LIMIT 2;
```

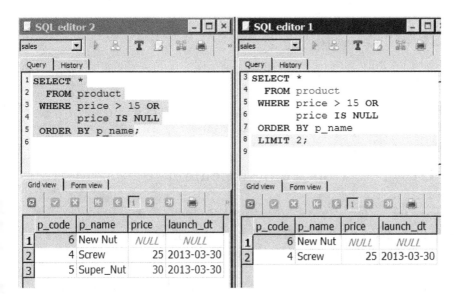

The DISTINCT Keyword

A query may return duplicate rows. Two rows are duplicates if each of their columns contains exactly the same data. If you don't want to see duplicate output rows, use DISTINCT in your SELECT clause. You can use DISTINCT on one column or multiple columns.

Using DISTINCT on A Single Column

The query in Example 3.13 uses DISTINCT on the price column.

Example 3.13: Using DISTINCT on a single column

```
SELECT DISTINCT price FROM product ORDER BY price;
```

Without DISTINCT, the query in Example 3.13 will return six rows that include two duplicate prices for row 3 and row 4, as shown on the right panel. Instead, the query in Example 3.13 returns five rows shown on the left panel.

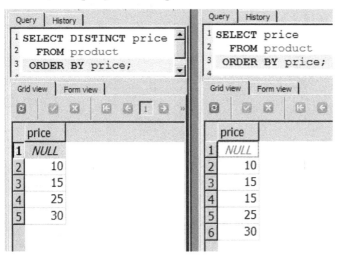

Aggregate Functions

You can manipulate your query output further by using aggregate functions. The aggregate functions are listed in Table 3.1.

Function	Description
MAX(column)	The maximum column value
MIN(column)	The minimum column value
SUM(column)	The sum of column values
AVG(column)	The average column value
COUNT(column)	The count of rows
COUNT(*)	The count of all rows including NULL.

Table 3.1: Built-in aggregate functions

As an example, the query in Example 3.14 uses the aggregate functions in Table 3.1.

Example 3.14: Using aggregate functions

```
SELECT MAX(price),
  MIN(price),
  SUM(price),
  AVG(price),
  COUNT(price),
  COUNT(*)
FROM product;
```

Note that COUNT(*) takes into account the New Nut product because though its price is NULL, while COUNT(price) does not.

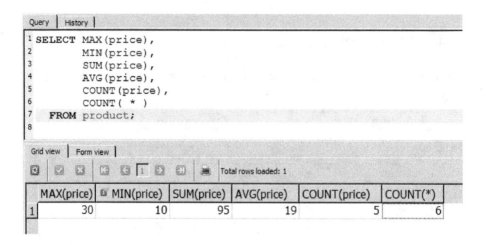

The CASE expression

CASE allows you to have dynamic query output in which a column value may vary depending on the value of the column. CASE comes in two flavors: Simple and Searched. Both will be explained in the following subsections.

Simple CASE

The general syntax for the Simple CASE is as follows.

```
SELECT columns,
  CASE column
    WHEN equal_value1
    THEN output_value1
    WHEN equal_value2
    THEN output_value2
    WHEN ...
    [ELSE else_value]
  END AS output_column
FROM table
WHERE ... ;
```

In the Simple CASE, *column_name* is compared to *equal_value*s in the WHEN clause, starting from the first WHEN and down to the last WHEN. If *column_name* matches a WHEN value, the value right after the THEN clause is returned and the CASE process stops. If *column_name* matches none of the WHEN values, *else_value* is returned if there exists an ELSE clause. If *column_name* matches none of the WHEN values but no ELSE clause exists, NULL will be returned.

As an example, the query in Example 3.15 uses a Simple CASE expression for the price column to produce a price_cat (price category) output column.

Example 3.15: An example of the Simple CASE

```
SELECT p_code,
  p_name,
  CASE price
    WHEN 10
    THEN 'Cheap'
    WHEN 15
    THEN 'Medium'
```

```
    WHEN 25
    THEN 'Expensive'
    ELSE 'Others'
  END AS price_cat
FROM product;
```

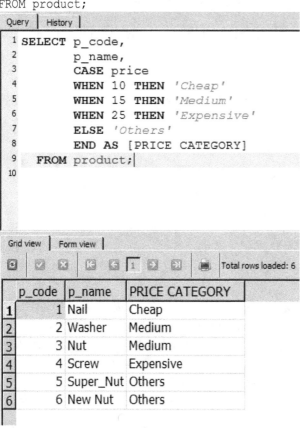

```
 1 SELECT p_code,
 2        p_name,
 3        CASE price
 4        WHEN 10 THEN 'Cheap'
 5        WHEN 15 THEN 'Medium'
 6        WHEN 25 THEN 'Expensive'
 7        ELSE 'Others'
 8        END AS [PRICE CATEGORY]
 9   FROM product;
10
```

Grid view | Form view

Total rows loaded: 6

	p_code	p_name	PRICE CATEGORY
1	1	Nail	Cheap
2	2	Washer	Medium
3	3	Nut	Medium
4	4	Screw	Expensive
5	5	Super_Nut	Others
6	6	New Nut	Others

Searched CASE

The case in the Simple CASE compares the equality of a column (price column in the example) with one or more values. On the hand, the case in the Searched CASE can be any condition. Here is the syntax for the Searched CASE.

```
SELECT columns,
  CASE
    WHEN condition1
```

```
    THEN output_value1
    WHEN condition2
    THEN output_value2
    WHEN ...
    ELSE else_value
  END AS output_column
FROM table
WHERE ... ;
```

The conditions are evaluated starting from the first WHEN and down to the last WHEN. If a WHEN condition is met, its THEN output_value is returned to the output_column and the CASE process stops. If none of the WHEN conditions is met, *else_value* is returned if there exists an ELSE clause. If no condition is met and no ELSE clause exists, NULL will be returned.

For instance, the query in Example 3.16 uses a Searched CASE. While the Simple CASE in Example 3.15 categorized the products based on only their prices, this Searched CASE categorizes the products based on the various conditions which can involve more than just the price. Note that in the Search CASE, NULL equality can be a condition that is not allowed in the Simple CASE.

Example 3.16: An example of the Searched CASE

```
SELECT p_code,
p_name,
CASE
 WHEN (price <= 10 AND p_name NOT LIKE 'Nut%') THEN 'Cheap'
 WHEN price BETWEEN 11 AND 25 THEN 'Medium'
 WHEN price > 25 THEN 'Expensive'
 WHEN price IS NULL AND launch_dt IS NULL THEN 'NA'
 ELSE 'Others'
END AS [PRICE CATEGORY]
FROM product;
```

```
Query │ History │
 1 SELECT p_code,
 2          p_name,
 3          CASE
 4          WHEN (price <= 10 AND
 5                      p_name NOT LIKE 'Nut%') THEN 'Cheap'
 6          WHEN price BETWEEN 11 AND 25 THEN 'Medium'
 7          WHEN price > 25 THEN 'Expensive'
 8          WHEN price IS NULL AND launch_dt IS NULL THEN 'NA'
 9          ELSE 'Others'
10          END AS [PRICE CATEGORY]
11     FROM product;
12
```

Grid view │ Form view │

Total rows loaded: 6

	p_code	p_name	PRICE CATEGORY
1	1	Nail	Cheap
2	2	Washer	Medium
3	3	Nut	Medium
4	4	Screw	Medium
5	5	Super_Nut	Expensive
6	6	New Nut	NA

Storing Query Output

You can store a query output into a new or existing table. To store a query output in a new table, use the following statement:

```
CREATE TABLE new_table AS SELECT ... ;
```

For instance, the query in Example 3.17 executes a SELECT statement and stores its result in a new table called nut_product. Query the nut_product to see if its nut rows are complete and correct.

Example 3.17: Storing output into a new table

```
CREATE TABLE nut_product AS
SELECT * FROM product WHERE p_name LIKE '%Nut%';
```

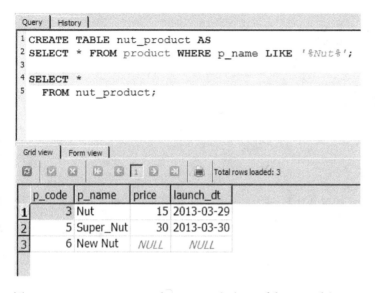

```
Query | History |
1 CREATE TABLE nut_product AS
2 SELECT * FROM product WHERE p_name LIKE '%Nut%';
3
4 SELECT *
5   FROM nut_product;
```

Grid view | Form view |

Total rows loaded: 3

	p_code	p_name	price	launch_dt
1	3	Nut	15	2013-03-29
2	5	Super_Nut	30	2013-03-30
3	6	New Nut	NULL	NULL

To store a query output into an existing table, use this syntax.

```
INSERT INTO existing_table AS SELECT ... ;
```

For example, the query in Example 3.18 stores the query result in an existing table.

Example 3.18: Storing output into an existing table

```
INSERT INTO non_nut
SELECT * FROM product WHERE p_name NOT LIKE '%Nut%';
```

Before executing INSERT statement of Example 3.18, first you have to create a non_nut table by executing the following statement.

```
CREATE TABLE non_nut
  (
    p_code     VARCHAR2(6),
    p_name     VARCHAR2(15),
    price      NUMBER(4,2),
    launch_dt  DATE,
    PRIMARY KEY (p_code)
  );
```

After running the query in Example 3.18, query the non_nut table and you should see the rows shown in the following screenshot.

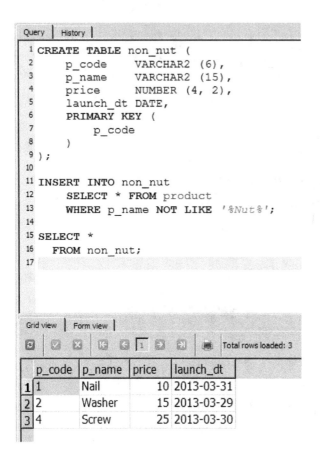

```
Query | History
1 CREATE TABLE non_nut (
2       p_code      VARCHAR2 (6),
3       p_name      VARCHAR2 (15),
4       price       NUMBER (4, 2),
5       launch_dt DATE,
6       PRIMARY KEY (
7            p_code
8       )
9 );
10
11 INSERT INTO non_nut
12      SELECT * FROM product
13      WHERE p_name NOT LIKE '%Nut%';
14
15 SELECT *
16   FROM non_nut;
17
```

Grid view | Form view

Total rows loaded: 3

	p_code	p_name	price	launch_dt
1	1	Nail	10	2013-03-31
2	2	Washer	15	2013-03-29
3	4	Screw	25	2013-03-30

Summary

SQL allows you to retrieve rows from a table and manipulate the output. You learned in this chapter that you can create aliases, column expression and various other techniques to produce output column.

Chapter 4 Grouping

A group is a set of rows having the same value on specific columns. In Chapter 3, "Query Output" you learned how to apply aggregate functions on all output rows. In this chapter you learn how to create groups of rows and apply aggregate functions on those groups.

The GROUP BY Clause

In a query the GROUP BY clause appears after the WHERE clause and before the ORDER clause, if any. Here is the syntax for a SELECT statement with the WHERE, GROUP BY, and ORDER BY clauses.

```
SELECT columns,
  aggregate_function(group_columns)
FROM table(s)
WHERE condition
GROUP BY group_columns
ORDER BY column(s);
```

As an example, the query in Example 4.1 groups the output from the product table by their launch date.

Example 4.1: Grouping on one column

```
SELECT launch_dt,
MAX(price) MAX,
MIN(price) MIN,
SUM(price) SUM,
AVG(price) AVG,
COUNT(price) COUNT,
COUNT( * ) AS [COUNT(*)]
FROM product
GROUP BY launch_dt;
```

The query output will have four rows (the right panel below), one for each of the four grouped launch dates. Note that the COUNT(price) element, which counts the rows with a value on their price column, produces 0. On the other hand, each COUNT(*) element, which counts the NULL launch dates, produces the count.

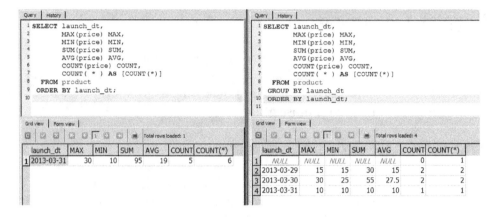

Grouping on more than one column

You can group by more than one column. If you do that, rows having the same value on all the columns will form a group. The query in Example 4.2 groups the rows by price and launch date.

Before you run Example 4.2, add a row using the following insert.

INSERT INTO product VALUES (9, 'Hammer', 25, '2013-04-01');

```
1 INSERT INTO product
2 VALUES (9,'Hammer', 25, '2013-04-01');
3
4 SELECT *
5   FROM product;
```

Grid view | Form view |

Total rows loaded: 7

	p_code	p_name	price	launch_dt
1	1	Nail	10	2013-03-31
2	2	Washer	15	2013-03-29
3	3	Nut	15	2013-03-29
4	4	Screw	25	2013-03-30
5	5	Super_Nut	30	2013-03-30
6	6	New Nut	NULL	NULL
7	9	Hammer	25	2013-04-01

Example 4.2: Grouping on two columns

```
SELECT price,
  launch_dt,
  MAX(price) MAX,
  MIN(price) MIN,
  SUM(price) SUM,
  AVG(price) AVG,
  COUNT(price) COUNT,
  COUNT(*) "COUNT(*)"
FROM product
GROUP BY price,
  launch_dt
ORDER BY price,
  launch_dt;
```

Even though the Screw and Hammer have the same price, they have different launch dates, and therefore form different groups, row 4 and row 5 on the output rows.

```sql
1 SELECT price,
2        launch_dt,
3        MAX(price) MAX,
4        MIN(price) MIN,
5        SUM(price) SUM,
6        AVG(price) AVG,
7        COUNT(price) COUNT,
8        COUNT( * ) [COUNT(*)]
9   FROM product
10 GROUP BY price,
11        launch_dt
12 ORDER BY price,
13        launch_dt;
14
```

Grid view | Form view |

Total rows loaded: 6

	price	launch_dt	MAX	MIN	SUM	AVG	COUNT	[COUNT(*)]
1	NULL	NULL	NULL	NULL	NULL	NULL	0	1
2	10	2013-03-31	10	10	10	10	1	1
3	15	2013-03-29	15	15	30	15	2	2
4	25	2013-03-30	25	25	25	25	1	1
5	25	2013-04-01	25	25	25	25	1	1
6	30	2013-03-30	30	30	30	30	1	1

HAVING Keyword

We use WHERE condition to select individual rows. On the other hand, the HAVING condition is used for selecting individual groups. Only groups that satisfy the condition in the HAVING clause will be returned by the query. In other words, the HAVING condition is on the aggregate, not on a column.

If present, the HAVING clause must appear after the GROUP BY, as in the following syntax.

```
SELECT columns,
  aggregate_function(group_columns)
FROM table(s)
WHERE condition
GROUP BY group_columns
HAVING aggregate_condition
ORDER BY columns;
```

As an example, the query in Example 4.3 uses the HAVING condition.

Before you run Example 4.3, please delete the Hammer using the following delete.

```
DELETE FROM product WHERE p_name = 'Hammer';
```

Example 4.3: Using the HAVING condition

```
SELECT price,
  launch_dt,
  MAX(price) MAX,
  MIN(price) MIN,
  SUM(price) SUM,
  AVG(price) AVG,
  COUNT(price) COUNT,
  COUNT(*) "COUNT(*)"
FROM product
GROUP BY price,
  launch_dt
HAVING COUNT(price) > 1
ORDER BY price,
  launch_dt;
```

Only groups having more than one row (satisfying the COUNT(price) > 1 condition) will be returned. Only one row will be returned, the one with price = 15 and launch date = 29-MAR-13.

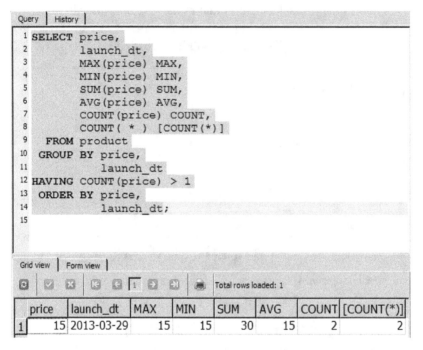

If a WHERE clause is present, it must appear before the GROUP BY clause. Individual rows will be selected by the WHERE condition first before grouping occurs. For instance, the query in Example 4.4 uses both WHERE and GROUP BY.

Example 4.4: Grouping with WHERE

```
SELECT launch_dt,
MAX(price) MAX,
MIN(price) MIN,
SUM(price) SUM,
AVG(price) AVG,
COUNT(price) COUNT,
COUNT( * ) [COUNT(*)]
FROM product
WHERE p_name NOT LIKE 'Super%'
GROUP BY launch_dt
HAVING launch_dt > '2013-03-29'
```

```
ORDER BY launch_dt;
```

The query on the left panel does not have WHERE condition; the right panel does.

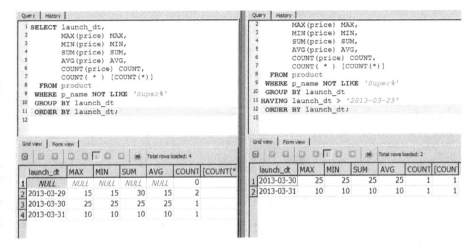

Summary

In this chapter you learned how to aggregate values from rows. You also learned to use the HAVING condition applied on aggregates. In the next chapter you will learn about the JOIN clause used to "aggregate" rows from more than one table.

Chapter 5 Joins

A real-world database typically stores data in dozens or even hundreds of tables. In these multi-table databases, a table often relates to one or some other tables. In this environment, you should be able to relate rows from two or more tables by using the JOIN clause. This chapter shows you how.

The syntax for the JOIN is as follows.

```
SELECT columns FROM table_1
JOIN table_2
ON table_1.column_1 = table_2.join_column_2
JOIN table_3
ON table_2.column_2 = table_3.join_column_3
JOIN …
;
```

Additional tables required for the examples

Please create the following three tables and add rows using the following SQL statements.

```
CREATE TABLE customer (
C_NO INTEGER PRIMARY KEY,
C_NAME TEXT
);

INSERT INTO customer
VALUES (10, 'Standard Store')
, (20, 'Quality Store')
, (30, 'Head Office')
, (40, 'Super Agent')
;

CREATE TABLE product (
p_code INT PRIMARY KEY,
p_name VARCHAR2 (10),
price NUMBER (10),
launch_dt DATE);

INSERT INTO product
VALUES (1, 'Nail', 10.00, '2013-03-31')
, (2, 'Washer', 15.00, '2013-03-29')
```

```
,  (3, 'Nut', 15.00, '2013-03-29')
,  (4, 'Screw', 25.00, '2013-03-30')
,  (5, 'Super_Nut', 30.00, '2013-03-30')
,  (6, 'New Nut', NULL, NULL)
;

CREATE TABLE c_order (
c_no INTEGER,
p_code INTEGER,
qty REAL,
order_dt DATE,
PRIMARY KEY (c_no, p_code, order_dt)
);

INSERT INTO c_order
VALUES (10, 1, 100, '2013-04-01')
,  (10, 2, 100, '2013-04-01')
,  (20, 1, 200, '2013-04-01')
,  (30, 3, 300, '2013-04-02')
,  (40, 4, 400, '2013-04-02')
,  (40, 5, 400, '2013-04-03')
;
```

Example 5.1 is an example of a JOIN query. It joins the rows from the c_order table to the rows from the customer table based on their c_no columns. The query returns the name of every customer who has placed one or more orders.

Example 5.1: A two tables join

```
SELECT c_name,
   p_code,
   c_order.qty,
   c_order.order_dt
FROM c_order
JOIN customer
ON c_order.c_no = customer.c_no;
```

```
1 SELECT c_name,
2        p_code,
3        c_order.qty,
4        c_order.order_dt
5   FROM c_order
6        JOIN
7        customer ON c_order.c_no = customer.c_no;
8
```

Grid view | Form view |

Total rows loaded: 6

	c_name	p_code	qty	order_dt
1	Standard Store	1	100	2013-04-01
2	Standard Store	2	100	2013-04-01
3	Quality Store	1	200	2013-04-01
4	Head Office	3	300	2013-04-02
5	Super Agent	4	400	2013-04-02
6	Super Agent	5	400	2013-04-03

Using Table Aliases

In a join query, different tables can have columns with identical names. To make sure you refer to the correct column of a table, you need to qualify it with its table. In the previous example, c_order.c_no (the c_no column of the c_order table) and customer.c_no (the c_no column of the customer_table) were how the c_no columns were qualified. A table alias can be a more convenient (and shorter) way to qualify a column.

For example, in the query in Example 5.2, o is an alias for the c_order table and c is an alias for the customer table. These aliases are then used in the ON clause to qualify the c_no columns with their respective tables.

Example 5.2: Using table aliases

```
SELECT c_name,
  p_code,
  o.qty,
  o.order_dt
FROM c_order o
JOIN customer c
```

```
ON o.c_no = c.c_no;
```

```
1 SELECT c_name,
2         p_code,
3         o.qty,
4         o.order_dt
5   FROM c_order o
6         JOIN
7         customer c ON o.c_no = c.c_no;
8
```

Grid view | Form view

Total rows loaded: 6

	c_name	p_code	qty	order_dt
1	Standard Store	1	100	2013-04-01
2	Standard Store	2	100	2013-04-01
3	Quality Store	1	200	2013-04-01
4	Head Office	3	300	2013-04-02
5	Super Agent	4	400	2013-04-02
6	Super Agent	5	400	2013-04-03

Joining More than Two Tables

From the JOIN syntax presented earlier, you can join more than two tables. To do this, in the SELECT statement, join two tables at a time.

For example, the query in Example 5.3 joins the c_order table to the customer table, and then joins the customer table to the product table. The rows in the c_order table are joined to the rows of the same c_no column from the customer table, and these rows are then joined to the rows with the same p_code from the product table. This query returns the customer names and their orders.

Example 5.3: A three table join

```
SELECT c_name,
  p_name,
  o.qty,
  o.order_dt
FROM c_order o
```

```
JOIN customer c
ON o.c_no = c.c_no
JOIN product p
ON o.p_code = p.p_code;
```

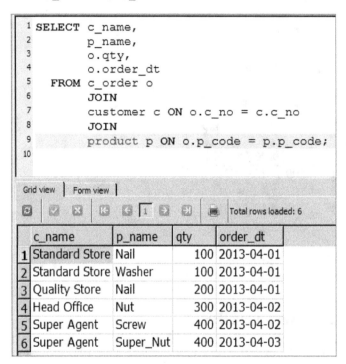

You can also apply WHERE conditions for selecting rows on a join query. For example, in Example 5.4, thanks to the WHERE condition, only products with names that do not start with "Super" will be in the query output.

Example 5.4: JOIN and WHERE

```
SELECT c_name,
  p_name,
  o.qty,
  o.order_dt
FROM c_order o
JOIN customer c
ON o.c_no = c.c_no
JOIN product p
ON o.p_code = p.p_code
WHERE p_name NOT LIKE 'Super%';
```

Executing the query in Example 5.4 against the sample tables will produce the following output rows.

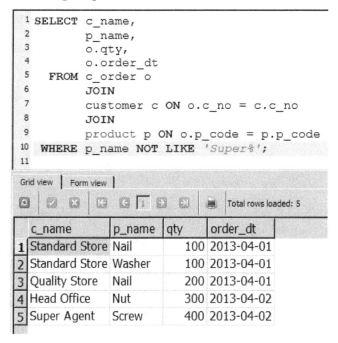

```
 1 SELECT c_name,
 2         p_name,
 3         o.qty,
 4         o.order_dt
 5   FROM c_order o
 6        JOIN
 7        customer c ON o.c_no = c.c_no
 8        JOIN
 9        product p ON o.p_code = p.p_code
10  WHERE p_name NOT LIKE 'Super%';
11
```

Grid view | Form view |

Total rows loaded: 5

	c_name	p_name	qty	order_dt
1	Standard Store	Nail	100	2013-04-01
2	Standard Store	Washer	100	2013-04-01
3	Quality Store	Nail	200	2013-04-01
4	Head Office	Nut	300	2013-04-02
5	Super Agent	Screw	400	2013-04-02

Joining on More than One Column

The preceding joins were on one column. Tables can also be joined on more than one column.

Before you try the next examples, please create the following shipment table and insert the rows using the following SQL statements.

```
CREATE TABLE shipment (
c_no INT,
p_code INT,
order_date DATE,
ship_qty INT,
ship_dt DATE
);

INSERT INTO shipment
VALUES (10, 1, '2013-04-01', 50, '2013-04-02')
, (10, 2, '2013-04-01', 100, '2013-04-02')
```

```
, (20, 1, '2013-04-01', 100, '2013-04-02')
, (30, 3, '2013-04-02', 300, '2013-04-03')
, (10, 1, '2013-04-01',  50, '2013-04-10')
;
```

The rows in the shipment table will be:

	c_no	p_code	order_date	ship_qty	ship_dt
1	10	1	2013-04-01	50	2013-04-02
2	10	2	2013-04-01	100	2013-04-02
3	20	1	2013-04-01	100	2013-04-02
4	30	3	2013-04-02	300	2013-04-03
5	10	1	2013-04-01	50	2013-04-10

To retrieve the order quantity (the qty column of the c_order table) of each shipment, you need to have a query that joins the shipment table to the order table on three columns, c_no, p_no, and order_dt, as shown in the query in Example 5.5.

Example 5.5: A multiple columns join

```
SELECT o.c_no,
   o.p_code,
   o.order_dt,
   ship_qty,
   ship_dt,
   qty
FROM shipment s
JOIN c_order o
ON s.c_no     = o.c_no
AND s.p_code   = o.p_code
AND s.order_dt = o.order_dt;
```

```
Query | History |
 1 SELECT  o.c_no,
 2          o.p_code,
 3          o.order_dt,
 4          ship_qty,
 5          ship_dt,
 6          qty
 7    FROM shipment s
 8         JOIN
 9         c_order o ON s.c_no = o.c_no AND
10                       s.p_code = o.p_code AND
11                       s.order_dt = o.order_dt;
12
```

Grid view | Form view |

Total rows loaded: 5

	c_no	p_code	order_dt	ship_qty	ship_dt	qty
1	10	1	2013-04-01	50	2013-04-02	100
2	10	2	2013-04-01	100	2013-04-02	100
3	20	1	2013-04-01	100	2013-04-02	200
4	30	3	2013-04-02	300	2013-04-03	300
5	10	1	2013-04-01	50	2013-04-10	100

Left Outer Join

All the joins I explained so far were inner joins. A LEFT OUTER JOIN query produces all rows from the table on the left of the left outer join will be in the output whether or not there are matching rows from the table on its right. The syntax for the left outer join is as follows.

```
SELECT columns
FROM table_1 LEFT OUTER JOIN table_2
ON table_1.column = table_2.column ... ;
```

Example 5.6 is an example left outer join query. This query returns all rows from the c_order table.

Example 5.6: Left outer join

```
SELECT o.*,
```

```
  ship_dt
FROM c_order o
LEFT OUTER JOIN shipment s
ON o.p_code = s.p_code
AND o.c_no   = s.c_no;
```

```
Query | History |
1 SELECT o.*,
2       ship_dt
3   FROM c_order o
4       LEFT OUTER JOIN
5       shipment s ON o.p_code = s.p_code AND
6                     o.c_no = s.c_no;
7
```

Grid view | Form view |

Total rows loaded: 7

	c_no	p_code	qty	order_dt	ship_dt
1	10	1	100	2013-04-01	2013-04-02
2	10	1	100	2013-04-01	2013-04-10
3	10	2	100	2013-04-01	2013-04-02
4	20	1	200	2013-04-01	2013-04-02
5	30	3	300	2013-04-02	2013-04-03
6	40	4	400	2013-04-02	NULL
7	40	5	400	2013-04-03	NULL

Note that the last two rows have no matching rows from the shipment table and therefore their ship_dt column has NULL values.

Rows with NULL only

If you want to query only orders that have not been shipped at all, you have to put this "only" condition in the WHERE clause of your query (ship_dt IS NULL) as in the query in Example 5.7.

Example 5.7: NULL only rows

```
SELECT o.*,
  ship_dt
FROM c_order o
LEFT OUTER JOIN shipment s
ON o.p_code = s.p_code
```

```
AND o.c_no  = s.c_no
WHERE s.ship_dt IS NULL;
```

Query	History

```
1 SELECT  o.*,
2          ship_dt
3    FROM  c_order  o
4          LEFT OUTER JOIN
5          shipment  s  ON  o.p_code = s.p_code  AND
6                           o.c_no = s.c_no
7 WHERE  s.ship_dt  IS  NULL;
8
```

Grid view	Form view

Total rows loaded: 2

	c_no	p_code	qty	order_dt	ship_dt
1	40	4	400	2013-04-02	NULL
2	40	5	400	2013-04-03	NULL

Self-Joins

Assuming some of your products have substitutes and you want to record the substitutes in the product table, you then need to add a column. The new column, which is called s_code in the product table, contains the product code of the substitute.

To add the s_code column, execute the following statement:

```
ALTER TABLE product ADD s_code integer;
```

Then, to update the p_code = 3 row, execute the following statement:

```
UPDATE product SET s_code = 5 WHERE p_code = 3;
```

The rows in the product table will now:

	p_code	p_name	price	launch_dt	s_code
1	1	Nail	10	2013-03-31	NULL
2	2	Washer	15	2013-03-29	NULL
3	3	Nut	15	2013-03-29	5
4	4	Screw	25	2013-03-30	NULL
5	5	Super_Nut	30	2013-03-30	NULL
6	6	New Nut	NULL	NULL	NULL

If you need to know the product name of a substitute, you need the query shown in Example 5.8. This query joins the product table to itself. This kind of join is called a self-join.

The syntax for the self join is as follows.

```
SELECT columns
FROM table alias_1
JOIN table alias_2
ON alias_1.column_x = alias_2.column_y;
```

Note that *column_x* and *column_y* are columns in the same table.

Example 5.8: A self-join

```
SELECT prod.p_code,
  prod.p_name,
  subst.p_code subst_p_code,
  subst.p_name subst_name
FROM product prod
LEFT OUTER JOIN product subst
ON prod.s_code = subst.p_code
ORDER BY prod.p_code;
```

Here are the output rows of the query, showing "Newer Nut" in the subst_name column of the third row.

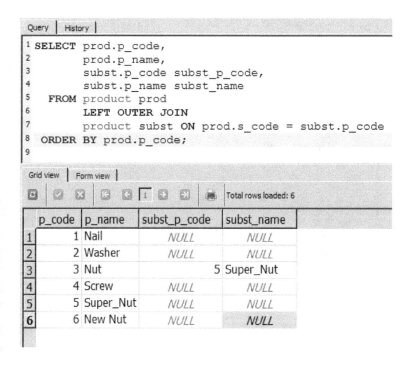

```
Query | History |
1 SELECT prod.p_code,
2        prod.p_name,
3        subst.p_code subst_p_code,
4        subst.p_name subst_name
5   FROM product prod
6        LEFT OUTER JOIN
7        product subst ON prod.s_code = subst.p_code
8 ORDER BY prod.p_code;
9
```

Grid view | Form view |

Total rows loaded: 6

	p_code	p_name	subst_p_code	subst_name
1	1	Nail	NULL	NULL
2	2	Washer	NULL	NULL
3	3	Nut	5	Super_Nut
4	4	Screw	NULL	NULL
5	5	Super_Nut	NULL	NULL
6	6	New Nut	NULL	NULL

The USING Keyword

A natural join will use all columns with the same names from the joined tables. If you want your query to join only on some of these identically named columns, instead of using the NATURAL keyword, use the USING keyword.

The syntax for joining two tables with USING is as follows.

```
SELECT columns
FROM table_1
JOIN table_2 USING (column);
```

Example 5.9, for example, joins the c_order table to the shipment table on only their p_code columns. It does not join the tables on their c_no columns. This query gives you the total quantity shipped by product code.

Example 5.9: USING

```
SELECT p_code,
  SUM(s.ship_qty)
FROM c_order o
```

```
JOIN shipment s USING (p_code)
GROUP BY p_code;
```

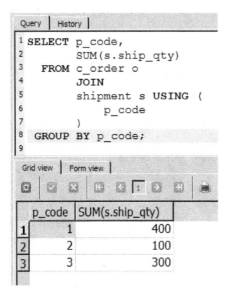

Summary

In this chapter you learned about getting data from multiple tables. You learned how to use join and its variations for this purpose.

Chapter 6 Compound Queries

You can combine the results of two or more SELECT statements using the UNION ALL, UNION, INTERSECT, or EXCEPT operators. The number of output columns from every statement must be the same and the corresponding columns must have identical or compatible data types.

This chapter shows you how to combine query results.

UNION ALL

When you combine two or more queries with the UNION ALL operator, the overall output will be the total rows from all the queries. For example, take a look at the query in Example 6.1. This query consists of two SELECT statements.

Example 6.1: Using UNION ALL

```
SELECT p_code, p_name, 'FIRST QUERY' query
FROM product p WHERE p_name LIKE '%Nut%'
UNION ALL
SELECT p.p_code,
  p_name,
  'SECOND_QUERY' query
FROM c_order o
INNER JOIN product p
ON o.p_code = p.p_code;
```

Note that the 'FIRST QUERY' and 'SECOND_QUERY' literals in the first and second SELECT statements, respectively, are just labels to identify where a row is coming from.

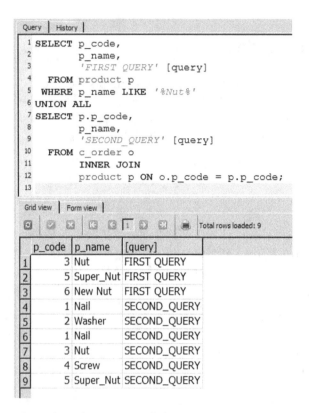

Note that the output of the query in Example 6.1 comprises all the records form the first SELECT statement followed by the rows from the second SELECT statement. You can of course use the ORDER BY clause to re-order this. For instance, the query in Example 6.2 modifies the query in Example 6.1 by ordering the results on the p_code column using the ORDER BY clause.

Example 6.2: Ordering output rows of a compound query

```
SELECT p_code, p_name, 'FIRST QUERY' query
FROM product p WHERE p_name LIKE '%Nut%'
UNION ALL
SELECT p.p_code,
  p_name,
  'SECOND_QUERY' query
FROM c_order o
INNER JOIN product p
ON o.p_code = p.p_code
ORDER BY p_code;
```

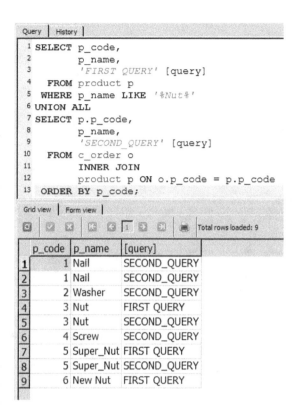

```
Query | History |
 1 SELECT p_code,
 2          p_name,
 3          'FIRST QUERY' [query]
 4    FROM product p
 5   WHERE p_name LIKE '%Nut%'
 6 UNION ALL
 7 SELECT p.p_code,
 8          p_name,
 9          'SECOND_QUERY' [query]
10    FROM c_order o
11          INNER JOIN
12          product p ON o.p_code = p.p_code
13   ORDER BY p_code;
```

Grid view | Form view |

Total rows loaded: 9

	p_code	p_name	[query]
1	1	Nail	SECOND_QUERY
2	1	Nail	SECOND_QUERY
3	2	Washer	SECOND_QUERY
4	3	Nut	FIRST QUERY
5	3	Nut	SECOND_QUERY
6	4	Screw	SECOND_QUERY
7	5	Super_Nut	FIRST QUERY
8	5	Super_Nut	SECOND_QUERY
9	6	New Nut	FIRST QUERY

UNION

UNION is similar to UNION ALL. However, with UNION duplicate rows will be returned once only. For example, consider the query in Example 6.3 that consists of two SELECT elements.

Example 6.3: Using UNION

```
SELECT p_code,
  p_name
FROM product p
WHERE p_name LIKE '%Nut%'
UNION
SELECT p.p_code,
  p_name
FROM c_order o
INNER JOIN product p
```

```
ON o.p_code = p.p_code
ORDER BY p_code;
```

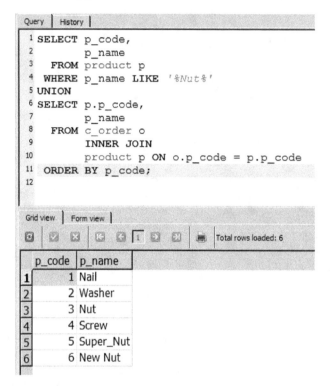

INTERSECT

When you combine two or more queries with the INTERSECT operator, the output will consist of rows common to all the participating SELECT statements. In other words, only if a row is returned by all the SELECT statements will the row be included in the final result.

Let's take a look at the example in Example 6.4.

Example 6.4: Using INTERSECT

```
SELECT p_code,
  p_name
FROM product p
WHERE p_name LIKE '%Nut%'
INTERSECT
```

```
SELECT p.p_code,
  p_name
FROM c_order o
INNER JOIN product p
ON o.p_code = p.p_code
ORDER BY p_code;
```

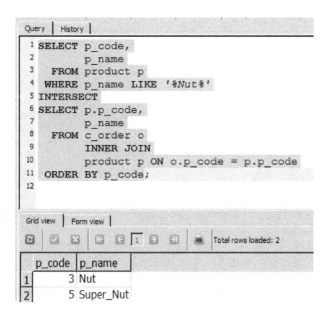

EXCEPT

When you combine two SELECT statements using the EXCEPT operator, the final output will be rows from the first query that are not returned by the second query. Take a look at the example in Example 6.5.

Example 6.5: Using EXCEPT

```
SELECT p_code,
  p_name
FROM product p
WHERE p_name LIKE '%Nut%'
EXCEPT
SELECT p.p_code,
  p_name
FROM c_order o
```

```
INNER JOIN product p
ON o.p_code = p.p_code
ORDER BY p_code;
```

```
 1 SELECT p_code,
 2         p_name
 3   FROM product p
 4  WHERE p_name LIKE '%Nut%'
 5 EXCEPT
 6 SELECT p.p_code,
 7         p_name
 8   FROM c_order o
 9         INNER JOIN
10         product p ON o.p_code = p.p_code
11  ORDER BY p_code;
12
```

p_code	p_name
6	New Nut

With EXCEPT, the order of constituting SELECT statements is important. If you swap the two SELECT statements in the query in Example 6.5, the output will be totally different. Take a look at the query in Example 6.6, which is identical to that in Example 6.5 except for the fact that the two SELECT statements have been swapped.

Example 6.6: Swapping the participating SELECT statements in a query combined with EXCEPT

```
SELECT p.p_code,
  p_name
FROM c_order o
INNER JOIN product p
ON o.p_code = p.p_code
EXCEPT
SELECT p_code,
  p_name
FROM product p
WHERE p_name LIKE '%Nut%'
ORDER BY p_code;
```

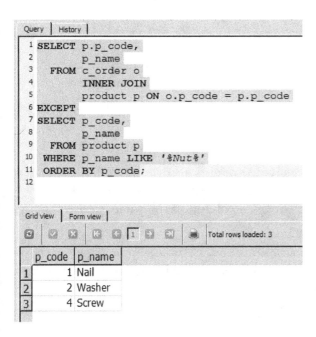

```
Query | History |
1 SELECT p.p_code,
2        p_name
3   FROM c_order o
4        INNER JOIN
5        product p ON o.p_code = p.p_code
6 EXCEPT
7 SELECT p_code,
8        p_name
9   FROM product p
10  WHERE p_name LIKE '%Nut%'
11  ORDER BY p_code;
12
```

Grid view | Form view |

Total rows loaded: 3

	p_code	p_name
1	1	Nail
2	2	Washer
3	4	Screw

Summary

In this chapter you learned that you can combine the output of two or more SELECT statements. There are five operators you can use for this purpose, UNION ALL, UNION, INTERSECT, and EXCEPT.

Chapter 7 Subqueries

A subquery is a query nested within another query. A subquery in turn can have a nested query, making it a multiple nested query. The subquery is also known as inner query; the enclosing query, outer query.

Single-Row Subquery

A single-row subquery is a subquery that returns a single value. A single-row subquery can be placed in the WHERE clause of an outer query. The return value of the subquery is compared with a column of the outer query using one of the comparison operators.

The subquery (printed in bold) in Example 7.1 returns the highest price among the prices of products that have been ordered. The outer query returns all products from the product table that have that highest price (in the example, 30.00), which is Super_Nut.

Example 7.1: A subquery returning a single value

```
SELECT *
FROM product
WHERE price =
  (SELECT MAX(price)
  FROM product p
  INNER JOIN c_order o
  ON p.p_code = o.p_code
  );
```

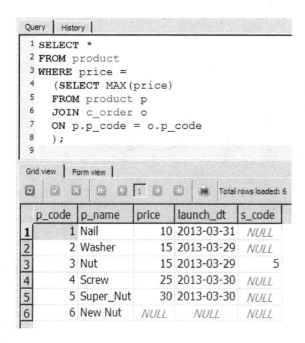

```
Query    History
 1 SELECT *
 2 FROM product
 3 WHERE price =
 4    (SELECT MAX(price)
 5    FROM product p
 6    JOIN c_order o
 7    ON p.p_code = o.p_code
 8    );
 9
```

Grid view | Form view

Total rows loaded: 6

	p_code	p_name	price	launch_dt	s_code
1	1	Nail	10	2013-03-31	NULL
2	2	Washer	15	2013-03-29	NULL
3	3	Nut	15	2013-03-29	5
4	4	Screw	25	2013-03-30	NULL
5	5	Super_Nut	30	2013-03-30	NULL
6	6	New Nut	NULL	NULL	NULL

The column and subquery result do not have to be the same column, but they must have compatible data types. In the query in Example 7.1, the price column of the product table is a numeric type and the subquery also returns a numeric type.

Multiple-row subquery

A subquery might return more than one row.

If, in Example 7.2 below, you select the subquery only and execute it by pressing F9, you will see its output has two rows, p_code 2 and 5. The first row, p_code 2, is picked (used) by the outer query.

```
Query | History |
1 SELECT *
2   FROM product
3 WHERE p_code = (
4                      SELECT p.p_code
5                          FROM product p
6                          JOIN
7                          c_order o ON p.p_code = o.p_code
8                      WHERE p.price BETWEEN 15 AND 20 AND
9                          p.price IS NOT NULL order by p.p_code
10               );
11
```

Grid view | Form view |

Total rows loaded: 2

	p_code
1	2
2	3

Example 7.2: Multiple-row subquery

```
SELECT *
FROM product
WHERE p_code = (
    SELECT p.p_code
    FROM product p JOIN c_order o ON p.p_code = o.p_code
    WHERE p.price BETWEEN 15 AND 20 AND
    p.price IS NOT NULL ORDER BY p.p_code
);
```

```
Query | History |
1 SELECT *
2   FROM product
3 WHERE p_code = (
4                      SELECT p.p_code
5                          FROM product p
6                          JOIN
7                          c_order o ON p.p_code = o.p_code
8                      WHERE p.price BETWEEN 15 AND
9                          p.price IS NOT NULL order by p.p_code
10               );
11
```

Grid view | Form view |

Total rows loaded: 1

	p_code	p_name	price	launch_dt	s_code
1	2	Washer	15	2013-03-29	NULL

First Row

If a subquery returns more than one row, as in Example 7.2 above, its outer query always picks up the first row. In Example 7.3, the order of the subquery output is now descending, meaning p_code 3 is the first row used by the outer query.

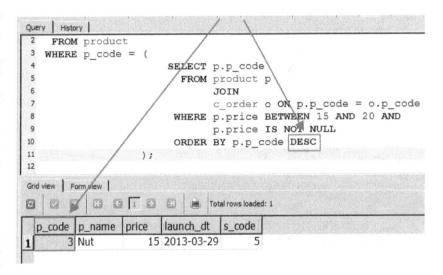

IN and NOT IN

If your outer query purposely intend to use all rows returning by the subquery, then use IN or NOT IN instead of = (equal to).

For example, the query in Example 7.3 contains a multiple-row subquery.

Example 7.3: IN subquery

```
SELECT * FROM product
WHERE p_code IN (
      SELECT p.p_code FROM product p
      JOIN c_order o ON p.p_code = o.p_code
      WHERE p.price BETWEEN 15 AND 20 AND
      p.price IS NOT NULL
      ORDER BY p.p_code DESC
);
```

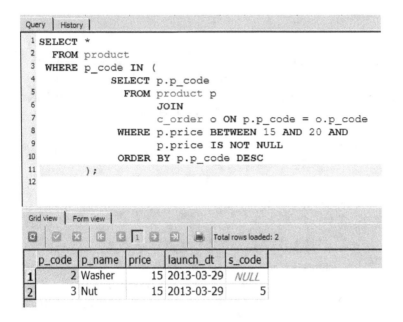

```
1  SELECT *
2    FROM product
3   WHERE p_code IN (
4            SELECT p.p_code
5              FROM product p
6                   JOIN
7                   c_order o ON p.p_code = o.p_code
8             WHERE p.price BETWEEN 15 AND 20 AND
9                   p.price IS NOT NULL
10            ORDER BY p.p_code DESC
11         ) ;
12
```

Grid view | Form view

Total rows loaded: 2

	p_code	p_name	price	launch_dt	s_code
1	2	Washer	15	2013-03-29	NULL
2	3	Nut	15	2013-03-29	5

Example 7.4 uses NOT IN. The result is, as expected, the products that are not there on result of Example 7.3.

Example 7.4: NOT IN subquery

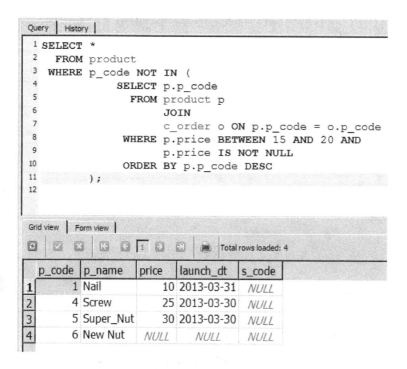

```
Query | History |
1  SELECT *
2    FROM product
3  WHERE p_code NOT IN (
4            SELECT p.p_code
5              FROM product p
6              JOIN
7                  c_order o ON p.p_code = o.p_code
8            WHERE p.price BETWEEN 15 AND 20 AND
9                  p.price IS NOT NULL
10           ORDER BY p.p_code DESC
11         ) ;
12
```

Grid view | Form view |

Total rows loaded: 4

	p_code	p_name	price	launch_dt	s_code
1	1	Nail	10	2013-03-31	NULL
2	4	Screw	25	2013-03-30	NULL
3	5	Super_Nut	30	2013-03-30	NULL
4	6	New Nut	NULL	NULL	NULL

Nested Subqueries

A subquery can contain a subquery as in Example 7.5. The whole query returns only customers who have not ordered any product having name that contains 'Nut'.

Example 7.5: Nested subqueries

```
SELECT customer.* FROM customer
WHERE c_no IN (SELECT c_no FROM c_order
                    WHERE p_code IN (SELECT p_code FROM product
                                WHERE p_name NOT LIKE '%Nut%'
);
```

| Query | History |

```
 1 SELECT customer.*
 2    FROM customer
 3  WHERE c_no IN (
 4             SELECT c_no
 5               FROM c_order
 6              WHERE p_code IN (
 7                       SELECT p_code
 8                         FROM product
 9                        WHERE p_name NOT LIKE '%Nut%'
10                    )
11        );
12
```

| Grid view | Form view |

Total rows loaded: 3

	C_NO	C_NAME
1	10	Standard Store
2	20	Quality Store
3	40	Super Agent

Correlated Subqueries

All the preceding subqueries are independent of their outer queries. A subquery can also be related to its outer query, where one or more column from the outer query table is (are) related to the column(s) of the subquery table in the WHERE clause of the subquery. This type of subquery is called the correlated subquery.

Let's add a customer using the following INSERT:

```
INSERT INTO customer VALUES(90, 'Choice Store') ;
```

Our customer table now has these five customers:

	C_NO	C_NAME
1	10	Standard Store
2	20	Quality Store
3	30	Head Office
4	40	Super Agent
5	90	Choice Store

We'd like to find the customers who have not placed any order. Having the correlated subquery, Example 7.6 accomplishes this. This subquery correlates the c_no of customer (from the outer query) to the c_no of the order (the subquery) as in the WHERE clause. The customer not having any order is the one we just added, Choice Store.

Example 7.6: Using a correlated subquery

```
SELECT customer.*
FROM customer
WHERE customer.c_no NOT IN (
      SELECT o.c_no
      FROM c_order o
      WHERE customer.c_no = o.c_no
);
```

Summary

In this chapter you learned subquery and its variations: nested and correlated. This is the last chapter of the book.

Appendix A: Command-line Shell

This appendix briefly introduces the Command-line shell tool that you can download from https://www.sqlite.org/index.html

Download the item highlighted in red below.

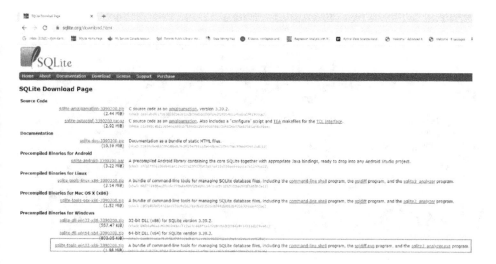

See screenshot below.

Start the Command-line shell from Windows command. Change to the folder where you want to store the database. Then enter sqlite3.

The Command-line shell is ready for your SQL activities, e.g. creating a database. You can enter SQL at the sqlite3> prompt, execute it by pressing Enter. The screenshot shows that you can create table, inserting data, and querying the data.

```
C:\Windows\system32\cmd.exe - sqlite3                              _ □ x

Microsoft Windows [Version 6.1.7600]
Copyright (c) 2009 Microsoft Corporation.  All rights reserved.

C:\Users\djoni>sqlite3
SQLite version 3.22.0 2018-01-22 18:45:57
Enter ".help" for usage hints.
Connected to a transient in-memory database.
Use ".open FILENAME" to reopen on a persistent database.
sqlite> .open sales.db
sqlite> create table product(p_code int, p_name text, price real, launch_dt text);
sqlite> insert into product values(1, 'Nail', 10, '2013-03-31');
sqlite> select * from product;
1|Nail|10.0|2013-03-31
sqlite> _
```

www.ingramcontent.com/pod-product-compliance
Lightning Source LLC
LaVergne TN
LVHW051712050326
832903LV00032B/4149